THE LOGICAL LEXICON OF USELESS ENGLISH

THESAURUS: A MAMMOTH BOOKWORM
(cf. Library lizard) (Endangered)

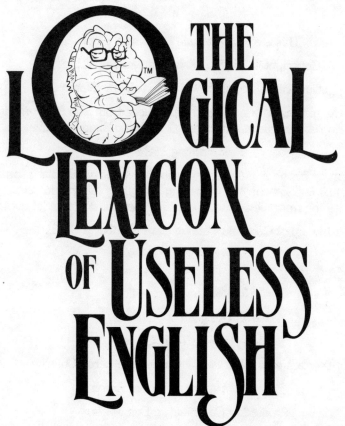

THE LOGICAL LEXICON OF USELESS ENGLISH

.....BEING A COMPENDIUM OF ETYMOLOGICAL ESOTERICA FOR THE EDIFICATION OF THOSE WHO WOULD RATHER LAUGH THAN LEARN

BY

WILLIAM WOOD

ILLUSTRATED BY

TONY GLEESON

A Note on the composition:

Cover Design: Tony Gleeson

Book Design: Tony Gleeson

Xerox Ventura Publisher® Consultant: Leroy Chen

Editorial Assistant: Kathleen Resch

Production Coordinator: Ben Martin

Typesetting and page formatting by computer using Xerox Ventura Publisher® and Microsoft Word® software

Typefaces used are Melior and ITC Souvenir

Printed and Bound in the United States of America by Gaylord Ltd. of Los Angeles, California

Pomegranate Press, Ltd.
3236 Bennett Drive
Los Angeles, California 90068

This book is dedicated to whoever will go for it.

William Wood has written novels, short stories, plays, poetry and movies for television, but this is the most preposterous thing he has ever done

Tony Gleeson currently purveys illustration and graphic design. His overriding ambitions are to remain sane and live long enough to be a burden to his children.

INTRODUCTION

In this book are many strange (and some not so strange) words, words that most people could live a long and fruitful life without ever seeing or caring to see. Yet, despite their obscurity, their sometimes shy demeanor or awkward appearance, these words are legitimate members of the English language and are, it seems to me, entitled to their moment in the limelight however brief. The difficulty, however, is that oftentimes their meanings are even more obscure and cumbersome than the words themselves and provide an important clue to our reluctance to use them. How often, for example, are we moved to speak of "any of various smaller species of bustards", which is the proposterous definition of the word "florican", when we don't even know what the hell a bustard* is? Common sense and a minimal knowledge of etymology would tell any reasonable person that a "florican" is a can to put flowers in - hence, a vase. Or, how many of us, at a social gathering, burst with desire to discuss "a grit or sandstone, unusually dark, containing feldspar**, fragments of rock such as slate or schist, various dark minerals, and interstitial clay"? This is the forlorn tonnage that the word "graywacke" has been lugging around for centuries. No wonder it has never gotten anywhere. If, however, the word had been assigned its obvious meaning - "an old lunatic" - the word would be guaranteed a much more useful and pleasant life; it would probably come up about as often as "frontispiece" (an athletic supporter) in polite conversation.

Hence, the rationale for this book. Save those words from their dreary life of obscurity by assigning them the meanings they clearly <u>should</u> have, as opposed to the ones that they <u>do</u> have. Following each word you will find the former. For the latter, you will have to look in the back. All "real" definitions are taken from the 1966 edition of the **Random House Dictionary of the English Language**, a most valuable volume which, because of its vintage, contains many words so obscure and peculiar that they are, in fact, teetering on the edge of extinction.

William Wood

* Look in the "B's"

** Look in the "F's"

ABUTMENT

ABORIGINAL	A copy
ABUTMENT	A huge ashtray
ACCUMBENT	Out of office
ACUMEN	Sharpshooters
ADAMSITE	The Garden of Eden
ADDUCE	To put on weight
ADHERE	Coming

ADMINISTER	Divinity student
ADVERT	To turn green
AFTERMATH	College
AGENTIVE	Male hormone
ALBUMEN	Caucasians
ALDERMAN	Tree surgeon
ALEATORY	Brewery
ANALOGIZE	To break wind
ANALOGUE	Two people breaking wind

ANALOGIZE

ANAPEST	Bug spray
ANCHORITE	Seaman (esp. lower grades)
ARMATURE	Semi-professional
AUTOCLAVE	Motel
AUTOCRACY	Detroit, Mich.
AUTOTOXIN	Carbon monoxide
AXILEMMA	The troubles surrounding Lizzie Borden

BARBELLATE

BEHEMOTH

B

BALDRIC	Toupee
BALLISTICS	Urology
BARBARISM	An atrocious haircut
BARBELLATE	Weight-lifter
BARBERRY	Peanut
BAROMETER	Shot glass
BASCULE	An illegitimate infant

BASILICA	Kitty litter (lit. coarse sand)
BAS-RELIEF	Privy
BATHYSPHERE	A round swimming pool
BEHEMOTH	A giant butterfly
BELLICOSE	Ulcer-prone
BELLWETHER	Nice day
BESTIALIZE	To improve
BIBLIOPHILE	Bookie
BICAMERAL	Tourist-like

BICORNE

BODKIN

BICORNE	A trumpet duet
BILLET	A low charge
BLUNDERBUSS	A clumsy embrace
BODKIN	Pygmy
BRATTICE	Kindergarten
BRONCHITIS	Saddle-sores
BUSTARD	Cop

C

CABALA	A large taxi
CABARET	A small taxi
CABOSHED	To be hit by a taxi
CADMIUM (Lat.)	My husband
CALAMARY	Species of *cannabis sativa* native to Southern Pacific States
CALORECEPTOR	Turkish bath

CALORIFIC

CAREEN

CALORIFIC	Obese
CAMPANILE	A transvestite
CARDIAC	A gambler
CAREEN	Woman driver
CARNIVORE	Sports car
CAROB	A stolen car
CAROON	An old car
CAROTID	A very old car

CARPOPHAGOUS	Hearse
CARPOPHORE	Student driver
CATENOID	A skunk
CAVENDISH	Bathtub
CELANDINE	Basement restaurant
CENTENARY	Broke
CENTIGRADE	Income tax
CENTIMETER	Budget
CHAMBERLAIN	Asleep

CAVENDISH

CENTIGRADE

CHANCERY	Las Vegas
CHANCELLOR	The Mayor of Las Vegas
CHAPFALLEN	An injured cricket player
CHARTREUSE	Map-maker (fem.)
CHICORY	Girls' dormitory
CHORTLE	An easy chore

CHROMINANCE	What makes one car worth more than another
CHROMITE	A compact car
CHROMOMERE	A low-priced car
CHROMOSOME	A medium-priced car
CHRYSELEPHANTINE	The Imperial

CHAPFALLEN

CICERONE	Member of the Capone gang
CINQUEFOIL	Fencing team
CODPIECE	Fish cake
COGENT	Best man
COMPUNCTION	Two flat tires
CONFIGURATION	(art.) Life class
CONJOINT	Adjoining bars

COMPUNCTION

CORNUCOPIA

COPIOUS	Assistant parson
COPREMIA	Police brutality
COPROPHOBIA	An extreme interest in police brutality (ref. ACLU)
COPULATE	To enroll in police academy
CORNUCOPIA (Med.)	Afflicted with many bunions
COTILLION	A billion trillions
CRANNY	Shrunken head
CREDULOUS	In debt

CRIBBAGE	Infancy
ROUGHAGE	Adolescence
TALLAGE	Maturity
SLIPPAGE	Middle age
PILLAGE	Old age
POSTAGE	Death

CRINOSE	Handkerchief

CROUPIER	Someone who coughs a lot

CUL-DE-SAC	Purse snatcher

CRANNY

CURFEW	Chiropractor
CURSORY	Men's locker room
CYCLAMEN	Hell's Angels (Pl. of *cyclone)*
CYCLOPEDIA	A sexually compliant woman (lit. *roundheels)*

D

DAMSON	Male lamb
DATIVE	Eligible
DECADENT	Bad teeth
DECUSSATE	To censor
DEMIJOHN	Bedpan
DEMONIAC	Embezzler
DEPLOY	To fire

DEPLOY

DERACINATION	Integration
DESINENCE	Obscurity
DESMID	Oasis
DEWLAP	Diaper
DIALECTIC	Character actor
DIALYSIS	Fear of telephones
DIAPAUSE	Period between children
DIATRIBE	Indian children

DIFFIDENT	False teeth
DILETTANTE	Having two aunts
DISABUSE	To apologize
DISGRUNTLE	To speak clearly
DOGMA	Bitch
DUNNITE	Bill collector

DIFFIDENT

ELUTRIATOR

E

EFFRONTERY	Brassiere department
ELLIPSIS	Trench mouth
ELUTRIATOR	Guitarist
EMBARGO	Bouncer
EMBOSS	To go into business for oneself

EMPTOR	Garbage collector
PREEMPTOR	Apprentice garbage collector
EPIGENE	A connoisseur of pork
ERRANT	Delivery boy
EWER	Lonely shepherd
EXCARDINATION	To be dropped by the Diner's Club
EXCOMMUNICATE	To hang up the phone
EXCULPATE	To cut hair

EMPTOR

49

EXEAT	To diet
EXPECTORATION	After dinner speech
EXPISCATE	To sit through an after dinner speech
EXTRAVERSION	Crib notes

EPIGENE

FASTUOUS

F

FALSEHOOD	Stool pigeon
FARADISE	Hell
FARTHINGALE	Cheap beer
FASTUOUS	Emaciated
FELDSPAR	Punchy fighter
FEMUR	Chastity belt
FETICIDE	Deodorant

FIBROID	A liar
FIBULA	Nineteenth hole
FILIBUSTER	A spanking
FINCA	Fink (fem.)
FINIAL	Aquarium
FIRKIN	A small Christmas tree
FISTULIZE	To pick a fight
FLAGELLATION	Patriotism
FLAGON (mil.)	Sunrise

FISTULIZE

FLAGRANT	Political speech
FLATULENT	Small-breasted
FLATUS	Weight watchers
FLORICAN	Vase
FLORID	Weed
FOULARD	Trichinosis
FRONTISPIECE	Athletic supporter
FUMITORY	Smoking section
FUNDAMENT	Bank vault

FLAGRANT

FUNGIBLE	Mouldy
FUNICLE	A joke
FUNICULATE	To tell a joke
FUNICULUS	Comedian
FURBELOW	Satyr
FURCATE	To appease one's wife
FURUNCLE	A wealthy, middle-aged man who spends freely on a young woman in return for her companionship or intimacy (cf. sugardaddy)
FURLONG	To desire a furuncle

GABELLE

GALAXY

G

GABELLE	Teen-age daughter
GAINSAY	Declared income
GALAXY	Chorus line
GALEASS	The end of a storm
GALYAK	Ladies' room
GAMBIER	Stocking salesman
GAMIC	Stacked

GAMMA	Marlene Dietrich
GANGLIATE	To join a gang
GANGLION	The boss
GANGLIONECTOMY	A change in command
GASTRULATE	To belch
GEMMATE	To become engaged
GEMMULE	A bachelor in favor of long engagements
GEMOT	Proposal
GIGAHERTZ	To go to work in a rented car

GASTRULATE

GLOSSAL

GIGLET	One day's work
GIGSMAN	Agent
GINGIVAL	Cocktail party
GINGIVITIS	Too many martinis
GLOSSAL	Floor wax
GOBLET	Sea Scout
GRAVAMEN	Undertakers
GRAYLAG	Hair dye
GRAYWACKE	An old lunatic

GREGALE	Tavern
GREGARINE	Barmaid
GRILLADE	Third degree
GRILLAGE	Police station
GRINDELIA	Comedienne
GROUNDSEL	Vacant lot
GUANINE	Female bat
GUAYULE	Santa Bat

GRAVAMEN

GREGARINE

GUMMOSIS	Loquacity
GUTTATE	To vomit

HABERDASHER	A well-dressed track star
HABITACLE	Nunnery
HABITUE	Nun
HABOOB	Novice
HACKBUT	Back of a taxi
HALOGEN	Saint
HALOGENATE	To canonize

HAYCOCK

HELLEBORE

HALOTHANE	A Scotch saint
HAMAN	Actor
HAMATE	Actor's wife
HAMMAL	Bad actor
HANAP	Forty winks
HAPLOSIS	Chronic optimism
HAPTICS	Jokes
HARL	Apprentice prostitute
HARTAL	Deer park

HAYCOCK	Hired hand
HELIAST	Sunbather
HELICAL GEAR	Bathing suit
HELIPORT	Beach umbrella
HELIX	Beach
HELLEBORE	Fundamentalist preacher
HEMATOBLAST	A bloody mess
HEMOLYSIN	A bloody shame

HEPTASTYLE

HEXAPOD

HEPTARCHY (obs.)	Jazz band
HEPTASTYLE	Be-bop
HEXACHORD	Wrong note
HEXANE	Witch hazel
HEXAPOD	Coven
HIPPOCAMPUS	The University of California
HISPID	Spaniard
HOCKET	Pawn shop

HYDRAGOGUE	Swimming teacher
HYDRATE	To swim
HYDRASTIS	Swimming badly
HYDRIDE	Speed boat

IMPANATION

INDIGOID

ILLAMON	Scottish doctor
ILLATION	Medicine
ILLATIVE	Physic
ILLUVIUM	Diarrhea
IMPANATION	Exorcism
INDIGES	Rich food
INDIGOID	A pauper

INDOLE	A lazy person
INDULT	Child
INQUILINE	Snub (as of the nose)
INTINCTION	Life
INTRADOS	Between the two of us
INVERSOR	Poet
ISOMORPH	Lonely man
ISOTONIC	One for the road

ISOTONIC

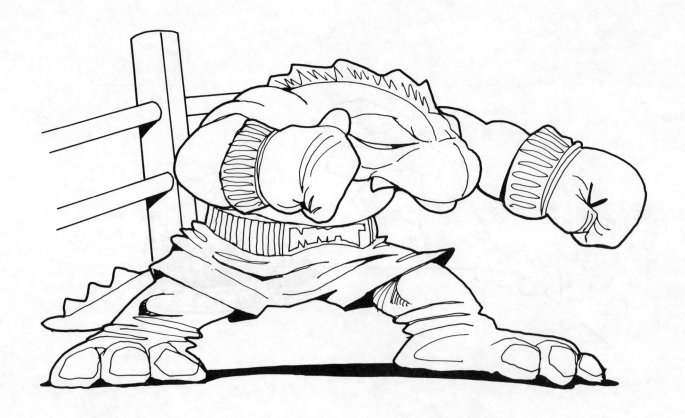

JABOT

JABOT	Boxer
JAVANINE	Afflicted with coffee nerves
JERKIN	Son-in-law
JETSAM	Flight mechanic
JETTON	Airline reservation
JUGAL	Single
JUGATE	To resist all temptation to marry

K

KALPIS	Hot water
KEGLER	Brew Master
KERNAL SMUT	Hardcore
KICKSHAW	Pedicab
KNOB LOCK	Tight Hat
KURTOSIS	Dog Breath

LAMPREY

LACUNOSE	Snotty
LAMBDOID	Meek
LAMPREY	Bulb-snatcher
LAPIDATE	Call-girl
LAYERAGE	Brothel
LIMBATE	Turkey bone
LIMPID	Cane

LIPECTOMY

LUXATE

LIPECTOMY	A close shave
LIPEMIA	An abnormal preoccupation with kissing
LIPOCHROME	Lipstick
LOCUTORY	Jail
LOPOLITH	A tall monument with the top gone
LORDOSIS	Delusions of grandeur
LOTUS	Big family
LOWBOY	Midget
LUXATE	To strike a match

LYMPH

A male nymph

LYMPHAD

The lymph olympics

MANATEE

MANDATE

MACAROON	A person with a Scottish grandparent
MACARONIC (Italian)	Stout
MAGPIE	A colossal pastry
MALACEOUS	Mischievous
MALANGA	Profanity
MALEBERRY	Testicle
MALKIN	Wife's relatives

MALLARD	Army food
MAMMOCK	Step-mother
MANATEE	Caddy
MANDATE	Gigolo
MANIC	Hairy
MANICURE	Depilatory
MANOMETER	Sperm count
MARGIN	A watery Martini

MELTON

MESODERM

MASTABA	The village idiot
MELTON	Ice cream cone
MENDACIOUS	Handy
MESODERM	Acne
MESOSPHERE	Smog
METASTABLE	Tack room
METHADONE	First attempt
MICROANGSTROM	A small Swede
MILLIGAL	Women's Army Corps

MILLIMHO	The Contra hearings (lit. a thousand laughs)
MINIMUM	Baby sitter
MISERICORD	Necktie
MITTIMUS	Applause
MONOCARPOUS	Having but one automobile
MONOSTROPHIC	Not so bad
MULIEBRITY	Stubbornness

MESOSPHERE

MISERICORD

MURRAIN	Wailing wall
MYOTOME	Autobiography

NASCENT	Odorless
NEPOTISM	Refraining from marijuana
NERVURE	Tranquilizer
NEURILEMMA	Whether or not to consult a psychiatrist
NIBLICK	Ponder (lit. to chew the pencil)
NICKELIFEROUS	Stingy
NICTITATE	To smoke

NERVURE

NICTITATE

NICTITATING MEMBRANE	Cigarette filter
NOCENT	Broke
NOMEN	Convent
NOMENCLATOR	Mother Superior
NOSOGEOGRAPHY	Middle of the face
NOSOPHOBIA	Suffering from chronic curiosity
NUDIBRANCH	Autumn
NUGATORY	Candy factory

NUDIBRANCH

O

OBTUND	Thin
OCTAD	(1.) Having eight children (2.) Crazy
OCTONARY	(1.) Person who has had eight heart attacks (2.) Corpse
ODOMETER	Nose
OLIVINE	The mock olive
OLOROSO	Rancid margarine

OMENTUM	Inertia
ONCOLOGY	The study of monogamous species (i.e., geese, wolves, etc.). obs., the study of man
ONEIROCRITIC	The New York Times' reviewer of plays
ONLAP	Toddler
ONLAY	How to get a toddler
ONTOGENY	Only child
ONTOLOGISE	How to get an only child

OMENTUM

ORTOLAN

OPALESCE	To acquire a friend
ORCHIDOTOMY	Broken date
ORDINAND	Man on the street
ORGANZA	Colossal debauch
ORTOLAN	Garbage disposal
OSTMARK	Dead letter
OSTRACOD	Lonely fish
OVERBANK	The Federal Reserve

OSTRACOD

P

PADDYMELON	An Irish grape
PALATALIZE	To call up a friend
PALET	Short friend
PALETOT	Childhood friend
PALINDROME	Fraternity house
PALINODE	Head of a friend
PALMATE	Ideal spouse

PALPUS	A rotten friend
PANDOUR	Of unpleasant mien (cf. sourpuss)
PANTLER	Tailor
PANTOLOGY	Art of the tailor
PAPABLE	Capable of reproduction (male)
PAPAVERACEOUS	Eager to reproduce
PARADIDDLE	Ready for sex
PARALLAX	Ready to lie down
PARAPET	Ready to acquire a dog

PALINODE

PARLANCE	Jack-knife
PARLAY	Premature ejaculation
PAROTIC	Imitative
PASSADO (football)	Quarterback
PASSAREE	Eligible receiver
PAS SEUL	Open receiver
IMPASSE	Interception
PATHOGENESIS	Trail-blazing
PATONCE	An unpredictable dog

PANTOLOGY

PASSADO

PASSAREE

PECCADILLO	An armored pig
PEDOCAL	Hot-foot
PEERAGE	Peep-show
PEERLESS	Blind
PENDRAGON	Famous writer (cf. literary lion)
PENEPLAIN	Hack writer
PENTOSE	Afflicted with writer's cramp
PENUMBRA	Pocket-sized parasol
PEPTIC	Active twitch

PECCADILLO

PEPTONE

PEPTONE	Loud sound
PERCUSS	Substitute for invective (cf. bleep, blankety-blank, etc.)
PERIAUGER	Outside chance
PERIWIG	Halo
PERMATRON	As Mother once said
PERNANCY	As Nancy once said
PERONEAL	As O'Neal once said
PERUKE	Part for ukulele

PERVERT	As Green once said
PESTLE	Flea circus
PETCOCK	Steady boy friend
PETROGLYPH	Picture of a dog
PETROUS	Afflicted with dogs
PETTIFOG	Mist
PHILOGYNY	Phil's kids
PHOTOPATHIC	Camera shy
PHOTOTAXIS	Camera stands

PERIWIG

PERUKE

PHYSIOCRAT	Jack La Lanne
PICRITE	Oddsmaker
PICROTOXIN	Long shot
PIERID	Bake sale
PILEATED	Afflicted with hemorrhoids
PILLION	Pharmacy
PINCHCOCK	Jockey shorts
PITCHPOT (baseball)	Catcher
PITCHSTONE	Bean-ball

PLANISPHERE	Flying saucer
PLUMBUM	Prune
PNEUMATOMETER	Bed-tester
POCOSIN	Indiscretion
POSTSCUTTLELUM	Lifeboat
POTATORY	Bathroom
PRELATE	On time
PRIMOGENIAL	Especially pleasant
PROFITEROLE	Function of an accountant

PHILOGYNY

PILEATED/PILLION

PROPINE	Policy of the Sierra Club
PUPARIUM	Dog house
PURPARTY	Tea dance
PURREE	Cat
PUTAMEN	Golfers
PUTLOG	Score card
PUTRESCENT	Having a lousy round
PUTTO	Inebriated golfer

PITCHPOT

PLANISPHERE

PRIMOGENIAL

PUTTO

Q

QUADRANT	Mini tantrum
QUADRIVIAL	Negligible (cf. trivial)
QUARTAN	Beige
QUATERNATE	Nate's grandchild

R

RACEMISM	Segregation
RACEMIZATION	Integration
RACEMOSE	Opposed to integration
RACEMULE	A fast ass
RADICAND	Victim of terrorism
RADICANT	Terrorist
RADICULAR	Fat terrorist

RAZZIA

RADIOGENIC	Blessed with a pleasant speaking voice
RADIOLARIAN	Evangelist
RAGWORT	Diaper rash
RANKET	Non-commissioned officer
RANKLE	Officer
RAPPEL	Bull session
RAPSCALLION	A bruised onion
RATINE	A female rodent
RATTAN	A brown rodent

RAZZIA	Violent argument
REBUFF	To undress again
REGLE	King
REGLET	Little king
REGMA	The king's mother
REGOLITH	The king's gravestone

RIBOSE/RIBOSOME/RIBOZO

RUBATO

RESIN	To play around
RESINIFEROUS	Filled with guilt
RESINIFY	To confess
RESINOUS	About to repeat the three previous steps
RESPONSORY	Advertising agency
RESPONSUM	Television show
RESTITUTION	Old age home
REVETMENT	Animal hospital
RIBOSE	Skinny

RIBOSOME	Sort of skinny
RIBOZO	Fat
ROLLICK	Stamp dispenser
ROSCOELITE	A little pistol
ROSEOLA	Juke box
RUBATO	Ripe tomato
RUBESCENT	Rural

S

SACKBUT	Boxer shorts
SAGITTARY	Brassiere
SALUTARY	Army post
SANITARIAN	Lavatory attendant
SANJAK	Jack, the lavatory attendant
SAPID	Dopey
SAPONIFY	To render dopey

SCARIFICATION/SCARIFICATOR

SAPROGENIC	Born dopey
SCARIFICATION	Horror
SCARIFICATOR	Horror movie
SCHIZOCARP	Half a fish
SCOLEX	Law school
SCOLOPENDRID	Law school dropout
SCOLOPHORE	Second year law student

SEMINATION	Small country
DISSEMINATION	Destruction of a small country, i.e. Vietnam
SEMITIC	Slight twitch
SEPTATE	To turn seven
SEPTILLION	Seventh birthday party
SEXAVALENT	To be acquainted with the *Kama Sutra*
SEXENARY	To be unacquainted with the *Kama Sutra*
SEXFOIL	Chaperone

SEXFOIL

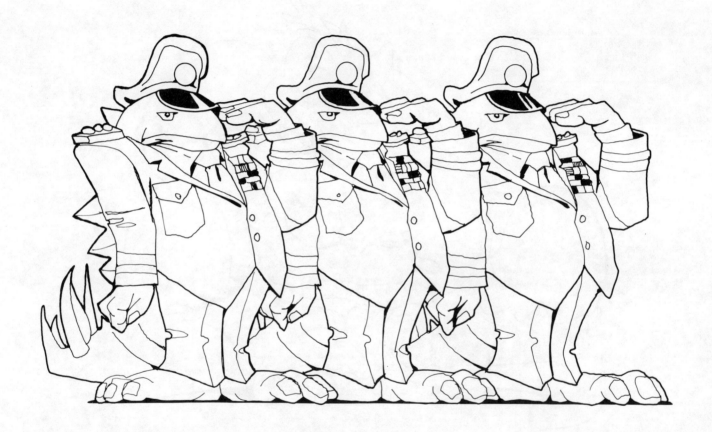

SHALWAR

SHALWAR	The Pentagon
SISKIN	Brother-in-law
SITULA	Chair
SMILACEOUS	Pleasant
SNIPPET	Poodle groomer
SPECTROGRAPH	Picture of a ghost
STAGGARD	A drunk
STANHOPE	Stan, Jr.
STATUTORY	Immobile

STENOTHERMAL	A very warm secretary
STENOTHERMOPHILE	An appreciator of very warm secretaries
STENOTOPIC	Wife
STEREOGRAM	Phonograph record
STERNUTATION	A scolding
STIGMATYPY	The National Enquirer
STINK HORN	Tail pipe
STONE CHAT	High conversation
SUBGUM	Chin

STAGGARD

SUCTORIAN

SUCTORIAN	Teacher's pet
SYLLABUB	(1.) Baby brother who has just learned to talk (2.) Pest
SYMPATHIN	Chamber music

T

TABLATURE	Stack of bills
TANGENT	Life guard (male)
TANGERINE	Life guard (fem.)
TARPAN	Ashtray
TECTRIX	Police woman
TELEPORT	Phone booth
TEMPLET	Shrine

TELEPORT

TRIODE

TENTORIUM	Abercrombie & Fitch
THESAURUS	A mammoth bookworm
THYMINE	Joint ownership
TITIVATE	To reach puberty (fem.)
TITUBATION	The act of deriving sexual pleasure by handling a small, grey bird
TOURMALINE	A bum trip
TRIODE	A poem that is three times longer than it should be
TRIPPANT	Passenger

U

UMBRETTE	Parasol
UNMORTISE	To resurrect
UNTOWARD	Stopped

V

VARIOCOUPLER	Dating service
VASTITY	Irreversible virginity
VOTARY	Poll tax

WARSTLE	Soldier
WHEELABRATE	To buy a new car
WINDAGE	Politician's speech
WIND SUCKER	Anyone who will listen to a politician's speech
WITHERITE	One who has grown old gracefully
WONDERBERRY	An upper

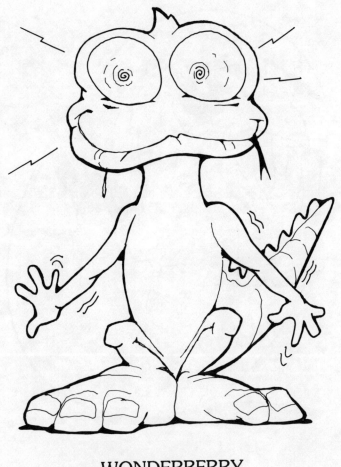

WONDERBERRY

YOKEFELLOW

Y

YAMPEE	A watery potato
YOKEFELLOW	A chicken

Z

ZED-BAR	After-hours club

GLOSSARY

All definitions in this glossary are selected and reproduced from the Random House
Dictionary of the English Language © 1966 by permission from Random House, Inc.

A

ABORIGINAL, adj. of or pertaining to aborigines; primitive.

ABUTMENT, n. *Archit., Civ. Eng.* a masonry mass supporting and receiving the thrust or part of an arch or vault.

ACCUMBENT, adj. reclining.

ACUMEN, n. superior mental acuteness and discernment.

ADAMSITE, n. *Chem., Mil.* a yellow irritant smoke, containing a poisonous form of arsenic, used as a harassing agent.

ADDUCE, v.t., to bring forward in argument as evidence.

ADHERE, v.i., to stick fast; cleave.

ADMINISTER, v.t., to manage (affairs, a government, etc.).

ADVERT, v.i., to remark or comment about or in relation to; refer.

AFTERMATH, n., that which follows or results from an event, esp. one of a disastrous or violent nature.

AGENTIVE, adj., *Gram.* pertaining to, or productive of, a form which indicates an agent or agency.

ALBUMEN, n., the white of an egg.

ALDERMAN, n., U.S. a member of a municipal legislative body; councilman.

ALEATORY, adj. *Law.* depending on a contingent event.

ANALOGIZE, v. to make use of analogy in reasoning, argument, etc.

ANALOGUE, n. something having analogy to something else.

ANAPEST, n. *Pros.* a foot of three syllables, two short followed by one long in quantitative meter, and two unstressed followed by one stressed in accentual meter.

ANCHORITE, n. one who has retired to a solitary place for a life of religious seclusion.

ARMATURE, n. 1. armor. 2. *Biol.* the protective covering of an animal or plant. 3. *Elect.* the part of an electric machine which includes the main current-carrying winding and in which the electromotive force is induced.

AUTOCLAVE, n. a heavy vessel in which chemical reactions take place under high pressure.

AUTOCRACY, n. uncontrolled or unlimited authority over others, invested in a single person.

AUTOTOXIN n. *Pathol.* a toxin or poisonous principle formed within the body and acting against it.

AXILEMMA, n. *Anat.* the membrane surrounding the axis cylinder of a nerve fiber.

B

BALDRIC, n. a belt, sometimes richly ornamented, supporting a sword, horn, etc.

BALLISTICS, n. the science or study of the motion of projectiles.

BARBARISM, n. a barbarous or uncivilized state or condition.

BARBELLATE, adj. *Bot., Zool.*, having short, stiff hairs.

BARBERRY, n. a shrub of the genus *Berberis*.

BAROMETER, n. *Meteorol.* any instrument that measures atmospheric pressure.

BASCULE, n. *Civ. Eng.* a device operating like a balance or seesaw.

BASILICA, n. (in ancient Rome) a large oblong building used as a hall of justice and public meeting place.

BAS-RELIEF, n. relief sculpture in which the figures project slightly from the background.

BATHYSPHERE, n. *Oceanog.* a spherical diving apparatus from which to study deep-sea life.

BEHEMOTH, n. an animal, perhaps the hippopotamus, mentioned in Job 40:15-24.

BELLICOSE, adj. inclined or eager to fight.

BELLWETHER, n. a wether or other male sheep who leads the flock, usually bearing a bell.

BESTIALIZE, v.t. to make bestial or beastlike.

BIBLIOPHILE, n. one who loves or collects books.

BICAMERAL, adj. *Govt.* having two branches, chambers, or houses, as a legislative body.

BICORNE, n. a two-cornered cocked hat worn esp. in the 18th and 19th centuries.

BILLET, n. lodging for a soldier.

BLUNDERBUSS, n. a short musket of wide bore with expanded muzzle to scatter shot at close range.

BODKIN, n. a small, pointed instrument for making holes in cloth, leather, etc.

BRATTICE, n. a partition or lining, as of planks or cloth, forming an air passage in a mine.

BRONCHITIS, n. *Pathol.* inflammation of the membrane lining of the bronchial tubes.

BUSTARD, n. any of several large, cursorial, chiefly terrestrial birds of the family *Otididae*.

C

CABALA, n. a system of esoteric theosophy and theurgy developed by rabbis from about the 7th to the 18th centuries, reaching its peak about the 12th and 13th centuries, and influencing certain medieval and Renaissance Christian thinkers.

CABARET, n. a large restaurant with a dance floor and an elaborate floor show.

CABOSHED, adj. *Heraldry.* (of an animal, as a deer) shown facing forward without a neck.

CADMIUM, n. *Chem.* a white, ductile, divalent metallic element resembling tin.

CALAMARY, n. a squid.

CALORECEPTOR, n. *Physiol., Biol.* a receptor stimulated by heat.

CALORIFIC, adj. pertaining to conversion into heat.

CAMPANILE, n. a bell tower.

CARDIAC, adj. pertaining to the heart.

CAREEN, v.i. *Naut.* (of a vessel) to lean, sway, or tip to one side while in motion.

CARNIVORE, n. any chiefly flesh-eating mammal of the order *Carnivora*.

CAROB, n. a caesalpinaceous tree, *Ceratonia Siliqua*, of the Mediterranean regions.

CAROON, n. *Brit. Slang, Archaic.* a five-shilling piece.

CAROTID, *Anat.* -n. Also called **carotid artery**. either of the two large arteries that carry blood to the head.

CARPOPHAGOUS, adj. that eats fruit.

CARPOPHORE, n. *Bot.* a slender prolongation of the floral axis, bearing the carpels of some compound fruits, as in the geranium and in many umbelliferous plants.

CATENOID, n. *Geom.* the surface generated by rotating a catenary about its axis of symmetry.

CAVENDISH, n. tobacco that has been softened, sweetened, and pressed into cakes.

CELANDINE, n. a papaveraceous plant, *Chelidonium majus*, having yellow flowers.

CENTENARY, adj. of or pertaining to a period of 100 years.

CENTIGRADE, adj. divided into 100 degrees, as a scale.

CENTIMETER, n. one hundredth of a meter.

CHAMBERLAIN, n. an official charged with the management of a sovereign's or nobleman's living quarters.

CHANCERY, n. the office or department of a chancellor.

CHANCELLOR, n. the title of various important judges and other high officials.

CHAPFALLEN, adj. dispirited; chagrined; dejected.

CHARTREUSE, n. (*sometimes cap*) an aromatic liqueur made by the Carthusiasn monks at Grenoble, France.

CHICORY, n. a perennial plant, *Chichorium Intybus*, cultivated as a salad plant and for its root, which is used roasted and ground as a substitute for coffee.

CHORTLE, v.i. to chuckle or utter with glee.

CHROMINANCE, n. *Optics.* the different in color quality between a color and a reference color that has an equal brightness and a specified chromacity.

CHROMITE, n. *Chem.* a salt of chromium in the bivalent state.

CHROMOMERE, n. *Genetics.* one of the beadlike granules arranged in a linear series in a chromonema.

CHROMOSOME, n. *Genetics.* any of several threadlike bodies, consisting of chromatin, found in a cell nucleus, that carry the genes in a linear order.

CHRYSELEPHANTINE, adj. made of or overlaid with gold and ivory.

CICERONE, n. one who shows and explains the antiques, curiosities, history, etc., of a place; guide.

CINQUEFOIL, n. any of several rosaceous plants of the genus *Potentilla.*

CODPIECE, n. (in the 15th and 16th centuries) a flap or cover for the crotch in men's hose or tight-fitting breeches.

COGENT, adj. convincing or believable.

COMPUNCTION, n. a feeling of uneasiness or anxiety of the conscience caused by regret for doing wrong or causing pain.

CONFIGURATION, n. the relative disposition of the parts or elements of a thing.

CONJOINT, adj. joined together; united.

COPIOUS, adj. large in quantity or number; abundant.

COPREMIA, n. *Pathol.* poisoning due to the presence of fecal matter in the blood.

COPROPHOBIA, n. *Psychiatry.* an abnormal fear of feces.

COPULATE, -v.i. to unite in sexual intercourse.

CORNUCOPIA, n. *Class. Myth.* a horn containing food, drink, etc. in endless supply.

COTILLION, n. a lively French social dance originating in the 18th century.

CRANNY, n. a small, narrow opening in a wall, rock, etc.

CREDULOUS, adj. willing to believe or trust too readily, esp. without adequate evidence.

CRIBBAGE, n. a game at cards.

ROUGHAGE, n. 1. rough or coarse material. 2. food, as green vegetables, bran, and certain fruits, containing a high proportion of indigestible cellulose which stimulates peristalsis in the intestines.

TALLAGE, n. a tax paid by a feudal tenant to his lord.

SLIPPAGE, n. the act or an instance of slipping.

PILLAGE, -v.t. to strip of money or goods by open violence, as in war; plunder.

POSTAGE, n. the charge for the conveyance of a letter or other matter sent by mail.

CRINOSE, adj. hairy.

CROUPIER, n. an attendant who collects and pays the money at a gaming table.

CUL-DE-SAC. n. a street, lane, etc. closed at one end; blind alley.

CURFEW, n. an order establishing a specific time in the evening after which certain regulations apply.

CURSORY, adj. going rapidly over something, without noticing details; hasty.

CYCLAMEN, n. any low, primulaceous herb of the genus *Cyclamen*, having tuberous rootstocks and nodding white, purple, pink, or crimson flowers with reflexed petals.

CYCLOPEDIA, n. an encyclopedia.

D

DAMSON, n. the small dark-blue or purple fruit of a plum, *Prunus insititia*, introduced into Europe from Asia Minor.

DATIVE, *Gram. -adj.* (in certain inflected languages, as Latin and German) noting a case having as a distinctive function indication of the indirect object of a verb.

DECADENT, adj. characterized by decadence; decaying; deteriorating.

DECUSSATE, v.i. to cross in the form of the letter X; intersect.

DEMIJOHN, n. a large bottle having a short, narrow neck, and usually being encased in wickerwork.

DEMONIAC, adj. of, pertaining to, or like a demon.

DEPLOY, v.t. *Mil.* to spread out (troops) so as to form an extended front or line.

DERACINATION, v.t. to isolate or alienate (a person or persons) from a native or customary culture or environment.

DESINENCE, n. a termination or ending, as the final line of a verse.

DESMID, n. any of the microscopic freshwater algae belonging to the family *Desmidiaceae.*

DEWLAP, n. a pendulous fold of skin under the throat of a bovine animal.

DIALECTIC, adj. of, pertaining to, or of the nature of logical argumentation.

DIALYSIS, n. *Physical Chem., Physiol.* the separation of crystalloids from colloids in a solution by diffusion through a membrane.

DIAPAUSE, n.a period of quiescence during the development of insects and other arthropods, characterized by a cessation of growth in immature stages.

DIATRIBE, n. a bitter, sharply abusive denunciation, attack or criticism.

DIFFIDENT, adj. lacking confidence in one's own ability, worth or fitness; timid.

DILETTANTE, n. a person who takes up an art, activity, or subject merely for amusement, esp. in a desultory or superficial way.

DISABUSE, v.t. to free (a person) from deception or error; set right.

DISGRUNTLE, v.t. to put into a state of sulky dissatisfaction.

DOGMA, n. a system of principles or tenets.

DUNNITE, n. an ammonium picrate explosive used as a bursting charge for armor-piercing projectiles and in high-explosive shells;

E

EFFRONTERY, n. shameless or impudent boldness.

ELLIPSIS, n. *Gram.* the omission from a sentence of a word or words that would complete or clarify the construction.

ELUTRIATOR, n. a machine for separating the particles of mineral by elutriation.

EMBARGO, n.an order of a government prohibiting the movement of merchant vessels from or into its ports.

EMBOSS, v.t. to raise or represent (surface designs) in relief.

EMPTOR, n. a person who purchases or contracts to purchase; buyer.

PREEMPTOR, (definition for preempt), v.t. to acquire or appropriate before someone else.

EPIGENE, adj. *Geol.* formed or originating on the earth's surface.

ERRANT, adj. journeying or traveling, as a medieval knight in quest of adventure.

EWER, n. a pitcher with a wide spout.

EXCARDINATION, n. the transfer of a cleric from the jurisdiction of one bishop to that of another.

EXCOMMUNICATE, -v.t. to cut off from communion or membership, esp. from the sacraments and fellowship of the church by ecclesiastical sentence.

EXCULPATE, v.t. to clear from a charge of guilt or fault.

EXEAT, n. permission granted by a bishop to a priest to leave his diocese.

EXPECTORATION, n. the act of expectorating.

EXPISCATE, v.t. *Chiefly Scot.* to find out by thorough and detailed investigation.

EXTRAVERSION, n. the act of directing one's interest outward or to things outside the self.

F

FALSEHOOD, n. a false statement; lie.

FARADISE, to stimulate or treat (muscles or nerves) with induced alternating electric current.

FARTHINGALE, n. a hoop skirt or framework for expanding a woman's skirt, worn in the 16th and 17th centuries.

FASTUOUS, adj. 1. haughty; arrogant. 2. showy; ostentatious.

FELDSPAR, n. any of a group of minerals, principally aluminosilicates of potassium, sodium and calcium, characterized by two cleavages at nearly right angles: one of the most important constituents of igneous rocks.

FEMUR, n. a bone in the lower limb, extending from the pelvis to the knee.

FETICIDE, n. the act of destroying a fetus.

FIBROID, adj. resembling fiber or fibrous tissue.

FIBULA, n. the outer and thinner of the two bones of the leg, extending from the knee to the ankle.

FILIBUSTER, n. *U.S.* the use of an exceptionally long speech by a member of the minority in a legislative assembly to prevent the adoption of a measure generally favored or to force a decision almost unanimously disliked.

FINCA, n. an agricultural property in a Spanish-speaking country.

FINIAL, n. *Archit.* a relatively small, ornamental feature at the top of a gable, pinnacle, etc.

FIRKIN, n. a British unit of capacity usually equal to a quarter of a barrel.

FISTULIZE, v. *Pathol.* to form a fistula.

FLAGELLATION, the act of whipping or scourging.

FLAGON, n. a large bottle for wine, liquors, etc.

FLAGRANT, adj. outrageously glaring; noticeable or evident.

FLATULENT, adj. generating gas in the alimentary canal, as food.

FLATUS, n. an accumulation of gas in the stomach, intestines or other body cavity.

FLORICAN, n. any of various smaller species of bustards.

FLORID, adj. 1. reddish, ruddy or rosy. 2. flowery; excessively ornate.

FOULARD, n. a soft, lightweight silk, rayon, or cotton of plain or twill weave with printed design, for neckties, trimmings, etc.

FRONTISPIECE, n. an illustrated leaf preceding the title page of a book.

FUMITORY, n. any plant of the genus *Fumaria*, of the family *Fumariaceae*.

FUNDAMENT, n. the physical characteristics of a geographical region. 2. the buttocks.

FUNGIBLE, adj. *Law.* (esp. of goods) being of such nature or kind as to be freely exchangeable or replaceable, in whole or in part, for another of like nature or kind.

FUNICLE, n. *Bot.* the stalk of an ovule or seed.

FUNICULATE, adj. *Bot.* having a funicle.

FUNICULUS, n. *Anat.* a conducting cord such as a nerve cord, umbilical cord, etc.

FURBELOW, n. a festooned flounce, as on a woman's gown.

FURCATE, adj. 1. forked, branching.

FURUNCLE, n. *Pathol.* boil.

FURLONG, n. a unit of distance, equal to 220 yards or 1/8 mile.

G

GABELLE, n. a tax; an excise.

GAINSAY, -v.t. 1. to deny. 2. to speak or act against.

GALAXY, n. *Astron.* a large system of stars held together by mutual gravitation and isolated from similar systems by vast regions of space.

GALEASS, n. *Naut.* a sailing vessel used for trading and fishing along the Baltic and Norwegian coasts, generally ketch-rigged, sometimes with a square foresail set flying.

GALYAK, n. a sleek, flat fur made from lambskin or the pelt of a young goat.

GAMBIER, n. an astringent extract obtained from the leaves and young shoots of a tropical Asian rubiaceous shrub.

GAMIC, adj. *Biol.* sexual.

GAMMA, n. the third letter of the Greek alphabet.

GANGLIATE, adj. having ganglia.

GANGLION, n. *Anat.* a gray mass of nerve tissue existing outside the brain and spinal cord.

GANGLIONECTOMY, n. *Surg.* the excision of a ganglion.

GASTRULATE, v.i. *Embryol.* to undergo gastrulation.

GEMMATE, adj. having buds; increasing by budding.

GEMMULE, n. an asexually produced mass of cells that will develop into an animal.

GEMOT, n. (in Anglo-Saxon England) a legislative or judicial assembly.

GIGAHERTZ, n. one billion hertz.

GIGLET, n. a giddy, playful girl.

GIGSMAN, n. *Naut.* a seaman assigned to a gig.

GINGIVAL, adj. of or pertaining to the gums.

GINGIVITIS, n. *Pathol.* inflammation of the gums.

GLOSSAL, adj. of or pertaining to the tongue.

GOBLET, n. a drinking glass with a foot and stem.

GRAVAMEN, n. *Law.* the part of an accusation that weighs most heavily against the accused.

GRAYLAG, n. a common gray, wild goose, *Anser anser*, of Europe.

GRAYWACKE, n. a grit or sandstone, usually dark, containing feldspar, fragments of rock such as slate or schist, various dark minerals, and interstitial clay.

GREGALE, n. a strong, northeast wind that blows in the central and western Mediterranean area.

GREGARINE, n. a type of sporozoan parasite that inhabits the digestive and other cavities of various living invertebrates and produces cysts filled with spores.

GRILLADE, n. a dish or serving of broiled or grilled meat.

GRILLAGE, n. a framework of crossing beams used for spreading heavy loads over large areas.

GRINDELIA, n. any of the coarse, yellow-flowered asteraceous herbs of the genus *Grindelia*.

GROUNDSEL, n. the lowermost sill of a framed structure, esp. one lying close to the ground.

GUANINE, n. *Chem., Biochem.* a colorless, crystalline, water-soluble solid, $C_5H_5N_5O$, found in guano and occurring in the liver and pancreas of animals and in the scales of fishes.

GUAYULE, n. a bushlike, composite plant, *Parthenium argentatum*, of the southwestern U.S. and Mexico, the tissues of which yield a form of rubber.

GUMMOSIS, n. *Bot.* a pathological condition in certain plants, characterized by the excessive formation of gum.

GUTTATE, adj. *Biol.* resembling a drop; having droplike markings.

H

HABERDASHER, n. *U.S.* a dealer in men's furnishings, as shirts, ties, gloves, etc.

HABITACLE, n. a niche, as for a statue.

HABITUE, n. a habitual frequenter of a place.

HABOOB, n. a thick dust storm or sandstorm that blows in the deserts of North Africa and Arabia.

HACKBUT, n. any of several small-caliber long guns operated by a matchlock or wheel-lock mechanism, dating from about 1400.

HALOGEN, n. *Chem.* any of the negative elements fluorine, chlorine, iodine, bromine, and asatine, which form binary salts by direct union with metals.

HALOGENATE, v.t. *Chem.* to treat or combine with a halogen.

HALOTHANE, n. *Pharm.* a sweetish, volatile, slightly water-soluble, non-flammable liquid, CF_3CHBrC_1, used as an inhalation anesthetic.

HAMAN, n. a powerful prince at the court of Ahasuerus, who was hanged upon exposure of his plan to destroy the Jews.

HAMATE, *Anat.* adj. hook-shaped.

HAMMAL, n. (in the Middle East and Orient) a porter.

HANAP, n. a tall medieval or Renaissance goblet of metal or glass, having a cover and often highly decorated.

HAPLOSIS, n. *Biol.* the production of haploid chromosome groups during meiosis.

HAPTICS, n. the branch of psychology that investigates cutaneous sense data.

HARL, -v.t. to drag or pull (an object) along the ground.

HARTAL, n. (in India) a closing of shops and stopping of work, esp. as a form of passive resistance.

HAYCOCK, n. a small, conical pile of hay stacked in a hayfield while the hay is awaiting removal to a barn.

HELIAST, n. (in ancient Athens) a dicast.

HELICAL GEAR, n. a cylindrical gear wheel the teeth of which follow the pitch surface in a helical manner.

HELIPORT, n. a landing place for helicopters, often the roof of a building.

HELIX, n. a spiral.

HELLEBORE, n. any of several ranunculaceous herbs of the genus *Helleborus*.

HEMATOBLAST, n. *Anat.* an immature blood cell.

HEMOLYSIN, n. *Immunol.* a substance, as an antibody, which in cooperation with complement causes dissolution of erythrocytes.

HEPTARCHY, n. government by seven persons.

HEPTASTYLE, adj. *Archit.* having seven columns.

HEXACHORD, n. *Music.* a diatonic series of six tones having, in medieval music, a half step between the third and fourth tones and whole steps between the others.

HEXANE, n. *Chem.* any of five isomeric hydrocarbons having the formula C_6H_{14}, of the alkane series, some of which are obtained from petroleum.

HEXAPOD, n. an insect; a member of the class *Insecta*.

HIPPOCAMPUS, n. *Class. Myth.* a sea horse with two forefeet, and a body ending in the tail of a dolphin or fish.

HISPID, adj. *Bot., Zool.* rough with stiff hairs, bristles, or minute spines.

HOCKET, n. a technique in medieval musical composition in which two or three voice parts are given notes or short phrases in rapid alternation, producing an erratic, hiccuping effect.

HYDRAGOGUE, *Med.* -adj. causing the discharge of watery fluid, as from the bowels.

HYDRATE, n. *Chem.* any of a class of compounds containing chemically combined water.

HYDRASTIS, n. goldenseal.

HYDRIDE, n. a compound of hydrogen.

I

ILLAMON, n. *Australian.* hielamon.

ILLATION, n. act of inferring.

ILLATIVE, adj. of, pertaining to, or expressing illation.

ILLUVIUM, n. the material accumulated through illuviation.

IMPANATION, n. *Theol.* the doctrine that the body and blood of Christ are in the bread and wine after consecration.

INDIGES, n. a title applied to a Roman deified for service to his country.

INDIGOID, adj. of or pertaining to that group of vat dyes which have a molecular structure similar to that of indigo.

INDOLE, n. *Chem.* a colorless to yellowish solid, C_8H_7N, having a low melting point and a fecal odor, found in the oil of jasmine or clove, used in perfumery and as a reagent.

INDULT, n. *Rom. Cath. Ch.* a faculty granted, usually for a specific period of time or for a specific case, by the pope to bishops and others, permitting them to deviate from the common law of the church.

INQUILINE, n. *Zool.* an animal living in the nest or burrow of another animal.

INTINCTION, n. (in a communion service) the act of steeping the bread or wafer in the wine in order to enable the communicant to receive the two elements conjointly.

INTRADOS, n. *Archit.* the interior curve or surface of an arch or vault.

INVERSOR, n. an instrument for drawing a curve and its inverse simultaneously.

ISOMORPH, n. an organism which is isomorphic with another or others.

ISOTONIC, adj. *Physical Chem.* noting or pertaining to solutions characterized by equal osmotic pressure.

J

JABOT, n. a falling ruffle or cascade of lace, worn at the neck or the front of the waist by women and formerly by men.

JAVANINE, n. *Pharm.* a crystalline, water-soluble alkaloid obtained from cinchona bark, used in medicine as an agent for stimulating the stomach and as a substitute for quinine.

JERKIN, n. a close-fitting jacket or short coat, worn in the 16th and 17th centuries.

JETSAM, n. goods cast overboard deliberately, as to lighten a vessel or improve its stability in an emergency, which sink where jettisoned or are washed ashore.

JETTON, n. an inscribed container or token.

JUGAL, adj. of or pertaining to the cheek or the cheekbone.

JUGATE, adj. *Bot.* having the leaflets in pairs, as a pinnate leaf.

K

KALPIS, n. a form of the hydria.

KEGLER, n. a participant in a bowling game, as candlepins or tenpins.

KERNEL SMUT, *Plant Pathol.* a disease or sorghum and other grasses in which the grains are replace by the black spores of a smut fungus.

KICKSHAW, n. a tidbit or delicacy.

KNOB LOCK, a lock having a spring bolt moved by a knob or knobs, and a dead bolt moved by a key.

KURTOSIS, n. *Statistics,* the state or quality of flatness or peakedness of the curve describing the frequency distribution in the region about its mode.

L

LACUNOSE, adj. full of or having gaps or missing parts, as in a manuscript.

LAMBDOID, adj. having the shape of the Greek capital lambda.

LAMPREY, n. any eellike, marine or fresh-water fish of the group *Hyperoartia*.

LAPIDATE, v.t. to pelt with stones.

LAYERAGE, n. *Hort.* a method of propagating plants by causing their shoots to take root while still attached to the parent plant.

LIMBATE, adj. *Bot., Zool.* bordered, as a flower in which one color is surrounding by an edging of another.

LIMPID, adj. clear, transparent, as water, air, etc.

LIPECTOMY, n. *Surg.* an operation for removal of superficial fat.

LIPEMIA, n. *Med.* excessive amounts of fat and fatty substances in the blood.

LIPOCHROME, n. *Biochem.* any of the naturally occurring pigments that contain a lipid, as carotene.

LOCUTORY, n. parlor.

LOPOLITH. n. *Geol.* a mass of igneous rock similar to a laccolith but concave downward rather than upward.

LORDOSIS, n. *Pathol.* forward curvature of the spine.

LOTUS, n. any aquatic, nymphaceous plant of the genus *Nelumbo*, having shieldlike leaves and showy, solitary flowers usually projecting above the water.

LOWBOY, n. *U.S. Furniture.* a low chest of drawers on short legs.

LUXATE, v.t. to put out of joint; dislocate.

LYMPH, n. *Anat. Physiol.* a clear yellowish slightly alkaline, coagulable fluid, containing white blood cells in a liquid resembling blood plasma, that is derived from the tissues of the body and conveyed to the blood stream by the lymphatic vessels.

LYMPHAD, n. *Archaic.* a galley having a single mast.

M

MACAROON, n. a drop cooky made of egg whites, sugar, usually almond paste or coconut, and sometimes a little flour.

MACARONIC, adj. composed of or characterized by Latin words mixed with vernacular words or non-Latin words terminated in Latin endings.

MAGPIE, n. birds of Eurasia and North America having long, graduated tails, black-and-white plumage, and noisy, mischievous habits.

MALACEOUS, adj. belonging to the *Malaceae*, or apple family of plants.

MALANGA, n. a thick, fleshy-leaved herb, *Xanthosoma atrovirens*, of South America.

MALEBERRY, a spreading shrub, *Lyonia ligustrina*, of the eastern U.S., having leafless, white flowers in terminal clusters.

MALKIN, n. *Brit. dial.* an untidy, lewd woman.

MALLARD, n. a common wild duck, *Anas platyrhynchos*, from which the domestic ducks descended.

MAMMOCK, *Brit. dial.* -n. a fragment; a scrap.

MANATEE, n. any of several herbivorous, gregarious sirenians of the genus *Trichechus*, of West Indian, Floridian, and Gulf Coast waters, having two flippers in front and a spoon-shaped tail.

MANDATE, n.*Politics.* a command or authorization to act in a particular way on a public issue given by the electorate to its representative.

MANIC, adj. pertaining to or affected by mania.

MANICURE, n. a professional treatment of the hands and fingernails.

MANOMETER, n. an instrument for measuring the pressure of a fluid.

MARGIN, n. 1. a border or edge. 2. the space around the printed or written matter on a page.

MASTABA, n. an ancient Egyptian tomb, rectangular in plan, with sloping sides and a flat roof.

MELTON, n. a smooth, heavy woolen cloth, for overcoats, hunting jackets, etc.

MENDACIOUS, adj. false or untrue.

MESODERM, n. *Embryol.* the middle germ layer of a metazoan embryo.

MESOSPHERE, n. (in the classification of the earth's atmosphere by chemical properties) the region between the ionosphere and the exosphere, extending from about 250 - 650 miles above the surface of the earth.

METASTABLE, adj. *Metall.* chemically unstable in the absence of certain conditions that would induce stability, but not liable to spontaneous transformation.

METHADONE, n. *Pharm.* a synthetic narcotic drug.

MICROANGSTROM, n. one millionth of an angstrom.

MILLIGAL, n. a unit of acceleration, equal to one thousandth of a centimeter per second per second.

MILLIMHO, n. *Elect.* a unit of conductance equal to .001 mho.

MINIMUM, n. the least quantity or amount possible, assignable, allowable, etc.

MISERICORD, n. a room in a monastery set apart for those monks permitted relaxation of the monastic rule.

MITTIMUS, n. *Law.* a warrant of commitment to prison.

MONOCARPOUS, adj. *Bot.* having a gynoecium which forms only a single ovary.

MONOSTROPHIC, adj. consisting of stanzas or strophes all having the same metrical structure.

MULIEBRITY, n. womanly nature or qualities.

MURRAIN, n. *Vet. Pathol.* any of various diseases of cattle, as anthrax, foot-and-mouth disease, and Texas fever.

MYOTOME, n. *Embryol.* the part of a mesodermal somite contributing to the development of the skeletal muscles.

N

NASCENT, adj. beginning to exist or develop.

NEPOTISM, n. patronage bestowed or favoritism shown on the basis of family relationship, as in business and politics.

NERVURE, n. *Bot., Zool.* a vein, as of the wing of an insect.

NEURILEMMA, n. *Anat.* the delicate, membranous sheath of a nerve fiber.

NIBLICK, n. *Golf.* a club with an iron head the face of which has the greatest slope of all the irons.

NICKELIFEROUS, adj. containing or yielding nickel.

NICTITATE, v.i. to wink.

NICTITATING MEMBRANE, a thin membrane, or inner or third eyelid, present in many animals, capable of being drawn across the eyeball, as for protection.

NOCENT, adj. harmful; injurious.

NOMEN, n. (in ancient Rome) the second name of a citizen, indicating his gens, as "Gaius *Julius* Caesar."

NOMENCLATOR, n. a person who assigns names, as in scientific classification; classifier.

NOSOGEOGRAPHY, n. the study of the geographical causes and distribution of diseases.

NOSOPHOBIA, n.. *Psychiatry.* an abnormal fear of disease.

NUDIBRANCH, n. a shell-less, marine snail of the suborder *Nudibranchia*, having external, often branched respiratory appendages on the back and sides.

NUGATORY, adj. trifling; of no real value; worthless.

O

OBTUND, v.t. to blunt, dull, deaden.

OCTAD, n. a group or series of eight.

OCTONARY, adj. pertaining to the number eight.

ODOMETER, n. an instrument for measuring distance passed over, as by an automobile.

OLIVINE, n. a common mineral, magnesium iron silicate, occuring commonly in olive-green to grey-green masses as an important constituent of basic igneous rocks.

OLOROSO, n. a sweet, dark dessert sherry.

OMENTUM, n. *Anat.* a fold or duplication of the peritoneum passing between certain of the viscera.

ONCOLOGY, n. the branch of medical science dealing with tumors.

ONEIROCRITIC, n. an interpreter of dreams.

ONLAP, n. *Geol.* the advance of a sea beyond its former shore.

ONLAY, n. an overlay, esp. one in relief.

ONTOGENY, n. *Biol.* the development or course of development of an individual organism.

ONTOLOGISE, v.t. *Chiefly Brit.* to express in ontological terms.

OPALESCE, v.t. to exhibit a play of colors like that of the opal.

ORCHIDOTOMY, n. *Surg.* incision of a testis.

ORDINAND, n. *Eccles.* a candidate for ordination.

ORGANZA, n. a sheer rayon, nylon, or silk fabric constructed in plain weave, used in the manufacture of evening dresses, trimmings, etc.

ORTOLAN, n. the bobolink.

OSTMARK, n. a cupronickel coin and monetary unit of East Germany, equivalent to about .24 of a U.S. dollar.

OSTRACOD, n. any of numerous minute, marine and fresh-water crustaceans of the subclass *Ostracoda*, having the body enclosed in a hinged, bivalve shell.

OVERBANK, v.i. *Horol.* (of a lever escapement) to have the balance staff oscillate so greatly that the fork of the lever fails to engage with the ruby pin, which then returns and forces the end of the lever against one of the banking pins, thereby stopping the timepiece.

P

PADDYMELON, n. any of several small Australian wallabies.

PALATALIZE, *Phonet.* -v.t. to articulate as a palatal or with relatively more contact between the blade of the tongue and the hard palate, as in certain pronunciations of the *l*-sound in *million*.

PALET, n. *Heraldry.* a diminutive of the pale, about one half the usual width and often used in pairs.

PALETOT, n. a loose overcoat.

PALINDROME, n. a word, line, verse, etc. reading the same backward as forward, as *Madam, I'm Adam*.

PALINODE, n. poem in which the poet retracts something said in an earlier poem.

PALMATE, adj. shaped like an open palm or like a hand with the fingers extended, as a leaf or an antler.

PALPUS, an appendage attached to an oral part and serving as an organ of sense in insects, crustaceans, etc.

PANDOUR, n. a brutal, marauding soldier.

PANTLER, n. *Archaic.* the servant or household officer in charge of the pantry.

PANTOLOGY, n. a systematic view of all human knowledge.

PAPABLE, adj. suitable or not unlikely to become pope.

PAPAVERACEOUS, adj. belonging to the *Papaveraceae*, or poppy family of plants.

PARADIDDLE, n. a drum roll, esp. on the snare drum, in which the beat is struck by the left and right drumstick in succession.

PARALLAX, n. the apparent displacement of an observed object due to a change in the position of the observer.

PARAPET, n. any low protective wall or barrier at the edge of a balcony, roof, bridge or the like.

PARLANCE, n. a way or manner of speaking; vernacular; idiom: *legal parlance.*

PARLAY, U.S. -v.t. to bet (an original amount and its winnings) on a subsequent race, contest, etc.

PAROTIC, adj. *Anat., Zool.* situated about or near the ear.

PASSADO, n. *Fencing.* a forward thrust with the weapon while advancing with one foot.

IMPASSE, n. a position from which there is no escape.

PAS SEUL, *Ballet.* a dance performed by one person; dance solo.

PATHOGENESIS, n. the production and development of disease.

PATONCE, adj. *Heraldry.* (of a cross) split into three points at the end of each arm.

PECCADILLO, n. a petty sin or offense; a trifling fault.

PEDOCAL, n. a soil rich in carbonates, esp. those of lime.

PEERAGE, n. the rank or dignity of a peer.

PEERLESS, adj. having no equal; matchless; unrivaled.

PENDRAGON, n. the supreme leader: the title of certain ancient British chiefs.

PENEPLAIN, n. *Geol.* an area reduced almost to a plain by erosion.

PENTOSE, n. *Chem.* a monosaccharide containing five atoms of carbon.

PENUMBRA, n. *Astron.* the partial or imperfect shadow outside the complete shadow of an opaque body, as a planet, where the light from the source of illumination is only partly cut off.

PEPTIC, adj. pertaining to or associated with digestion; digestive.

PEPTONE, n. *Biochem.* any of a class of diffusible, soluble substances into which proteins are converted by partial hydrolysis.

PERCUSS, v.t. to strike (something) so as to shake or cause a shock to.

PERIAUGER, n. a flat-bottomed, leeboard sailing barge.

PERIWIG, n. a peruke or wig.

PERMATRON, n. *Electronics.* a thermionic gas diode in which the flow of electrons is controlled by an external magnetic field instead of a grid.

PERNANCY, n. *Law.* a taking or receiving, as of the rents or profits of an estate.

PERONEAL, adj. *Anat.* pertaining to or situated near the fibula.

PERUKE, n. a wig, esp. of the kind worn by men in the 17th and 18th centuries; periwig.

PERVERT, n., v.t. to turn away from the right course.

PESTLE, n. an instrument for braying or triturating substances in a mortar.

PETCOCK, n. a small valve or faucet, as for draining off excess or waste material from the cylinder of a steam engine or internal-combustion engine.

PETROGLYPH, n. a drawing or carving on rock, made by a member of a prehistoric or primitive people.

PETROUS, adj. *Anat.* noting or pertaining to the hard dense portion of the temporal bone, containing the internal auditory organs.

PETTIFOG, v.i. to bicker or quibble over trifles when more important matters are to be dealt with.

PHILOGYNY, n. love of or liking for women.

PHOTOPATHIC, adj. (of an organism) characterized by movement away from a source of light.

PHOTOTAXIS, n. *Biol.* movement of an organism toward or away from a source of light.

PHYSIOCRAT, n. one of a school of political economists who followed Quesnay in holding that an inherent natural order properly governed society.

PICRITE, n. a granular igneous rock composed chiefly of olivine and augite.

PICROTOXIN, n. *Pharm.* a white, crystalline, slightly water-soluble, bitter, poisonous solid, obtained from the seeds of *Anamirta cocculus.*

PIERID, adj. belonging to or pertaining to the *Pieridae*, a family of butterflies.

PILEATED, adj. *Ornith.* crested.

PILLION, n. a pad or cushion attached behind a saddle, esp. as a seat for a woman.

PINCHCOCK, n. a clamp for compressing a flexibile pipe, as a rubber tube, in order to regulate or stop the flow of a fluid.

PITCHPOT, n. a pot used by sailors for heating pitch.

PITCHSTONE, n. a glassy igneous rock having a resinous luster and resembling hardened pitch.

PLANISPHERE, n. a map of half or more of the celestial sphere with a device for indicating the part visible at a given time at a given location.

PLUMBUM, n. *Chem.* lead.

PNEUMATOMETER, n. an instrument for measuring either the quantity or force of air inhaled or exhaled during a single inspiration or expiration.

POCOSIN, n. *Southeastern U.S.* a swamp or marsh in an upland coastal region.

POSTSCUTTLELUM, n. postnotum.

POTATORY, adj. of, pertaining to, or given to drinking.

PRELATE, n. an ecclesiastic of a high order, as an archbishop, bishop, etc.

PRIMOGENIAL, adj. of a primitive type; primordial.

PROFITEROLE, n. a small cream puff with a sweet or savory filling, as of cream and chocolate sauce.

PROPINE, n. *Scot.* a present; gift.

PUPARIUM, n. *Entomol.* a pupal case formed of the cuticula of a preceding larval instar.

PURPARTY, n. *Law.* a share of an estate held by coparceners that is apportioned to one upon the division of the estate among them.

PURREE, adj. having the color Indian yellow.

PUTAMEN, *Bot.* a hard or stony endocarp, as a peach stone.

PUTLOG, n. any of the short horizontal timbers supporting the floor of a builder's scaffold.

PUTRESCENT, adj. becoming putrid; in process of putrefaction.

PUTTO, n. *Fine Arts.* a representation of a cherubic infant, often shown winged.

Q

QUADRANT, n. a quarter of a circle; an arc of 90 degrees.

QUADRIVIAL, adj. having four ways or roads meeting in a point.

QUARTAN, adj. (of a fever, ague, etc.) characterized by paroxysms that recur every fourth day.

QUATERNATE, adj. arranged in or consisting of four parts, as the leaves of certain plants.

R

RACEMISM, n. *Chem.* (of a compound) the state of being optically inactive and separable into two other substances of the same chemical composition as the original substance, one of which is dextrorotatory and the other leverotatory, as racemic acid.

RACEMIZATION, n. *Chem.* the conversion of an optically active substance into an optically inactive mixture of equal amounts of the dextrorotatory and leverotatory forms.

RACEMOSE, adj. *Bot.* having the form of a raceme.

RACEMULE, n. *Bot.* a small raceme.

RADICAND, n. *Math.* the quantity under a radical sign.

RADICANT, adj. *Bot.* rooting from the stem, as ivy.

RADICULAR, adj. *Bot.* of or pertaining to a radicle or root.

RADIOGENIC, adj. *Physics.* produced by radioactive decay.

RADIOLARIAN, n. any minute marine protozoan of the group or order *Radiolaria*.

RAGWORT, n. any of various composite plants of the genus *Senecio*.

RANKET, n. a double-reed wind instrument of the 16th and 17th centuries.

RANKLE, v. (of unpleasant feelings, experiences, etc.) to continue to cause keen irritation or bitter resentment within the mind.

RAPPEL, n. (in mountaineering) the act or method of moving down a steep incline by means of a double rope secured above and placed around the boy, usually under the left thigh and over the right shoulder, and paid out gradually in the descent.

RAPSCALLION, n. a rascal; rogue; scamp.

RATINE, n. a loosely woven fabric made with a nubby or knotty yarns.

RATTAN, n. any of various climbing palms of the genus *Calamus*.

RAZZIA, n. a plundering raid.

REBUFF, n. a blunt or abrupt rejection.

REGLE, n. a groove or channel for guiding a sliding door.

REGLET, n. *Archit.* a groove for guiding or holding a panel, window sash, etc.

REGMA, *Bot.* a dry fruit consisting of three or more carpels which separate from the axis at maturity.

REGOLITH, n. *Phys. Geog.* the layer of disintegrated and decomposed rock fragments, including soil, just above the solid rock of the earth's crust.

RESIN. n. any of a class of nonvolatile solid or semisolid organic substances, as copal, mastic, etc., obtained directly from certain plants as exudations or prepared by polymerization of simple molecules: used in medicine and in the making of varnishes and plastics.

RESINIFEROUS, adj. yielding resin.

RESINIFY, *Chem.* -v.t. to convert into a resin.

RESINOUS. adj. full of or containing resin.

RESPONSORY, n. *Eccles.* an anthem sung by a soloist and choir alternately.

RESPONSUM, n. the reply of a noted rabbi or Jewish scholar as used in the Responsa.

RESTITUTION, n. reparation made by giving an equivalent or compensation for loss.

REVETMENT, n. a facing of masonry or the like, esp. for protecting an embankment.

RIBOSE, n. *Chem.* a pentose sugar obtained by the hydrolysis of RNA.

RIBOSOME, n. *Biol.* (in the cytoplasm of a cell) any of several minute, angular or spherical particles that are composed of protein and RNA.

RIBOZO, n. a long woven scarf, often of fine material, worn over the head and shoulders by Spanish and Mexican women.

ROLLICK, v.i. to move or act in a careless, frolicsome manner.

ROSCOELITE, n. *Mineral.* a brown variety of muscovite having the aluminum partly replaced by vanadium.

ROSEOLA, n. *Pathol.* a kind of rose-colored rash.

RUBATO, adj., n. *Music,* -adj. 1. having certain notes arbitrarily lengthened while others are correspondingly shortened, or vice versa.

RUBESCENT, adj. becoming red, blushing.

S

SACKBUT, n. a medieval form of the trombone.

SAGITTARY, n. a centaur with a bow, as Chiron.

SALUTARY, adj. favorable to or promoting health.

SANITARIAN, adv. sanitary, clean, wholesome.n.

SANJAK, n. (in Turkey) one of the administrative districts into which a vilayet is divided.

SAPID, adj. having taste or flavor.

SAPONIFY, v. *Chem.* to convert (a fat) into soap by treating with an alkali.

SAPROGENIC, adj. producing putrefaction or decay, as certain bacteria.

SCARIFICATION, n. the act or an instance of scarifying.

SCARIFICATOR, n. one who scarifies.

SCHIZOCARP, n. *Bot.* a dry fruit which at maturity splits into two or more one-seeded indehiscent carpels.

SCOLEX, n. *Zool.* the anterior, headlike segment of a tapeworm.

SCOLOPENDRID, n. any myriapod of the order *Scolopendrida*, including many large, poisonous centipedes.

SCOLOPHORE, n. *Zool.* a sense organ in the body wall of insects that is sensitive to sound waves.

SEMINATION, n. a sowing or impregnating; dissemination.

DISSEMINATION, n. scattering or spreading wildly, as though sowing seed.

SEMITIC, n. an important subfamily of Afro-Asiatic languages, including Akkadian, Arabic, Aramaic, and Hebrew.

SEPTATE, adj. *Biol.* divided by a septum or septa.

SEPTILLION, -n. a cardinal number represented in the U.S. and France by one followed by 24 zeros and, in Great Britain and Germany, by one followed by 42 zeros.

SEXAVALENT, adj. *Chem.* having a valence of six.

SEXENARY, adj. 1. senary. 2. sextuple.

SEXFOIL, n. a round ornament consisting of six lobes divided by cusps.

SHALWAR, n. loose, pajamalike trousers worn by both men and women in India and southeast Asia.

SISKIN, n. any of several small cardueline finches, esp. *Spinus spinus*, of Europe.

SITULA, n. a deep urn, vase, or bucket-shaped vessel, esp. one made in the ancient world.

SMILACEOUS, adj. belonging to the *Smilacaceae*, the smilax or greenbrier family of plants.

SNIPPET, n. a small piece snipped off; a small bit, scrap, or fragment.

SPECTROGRAPH, n. a spectroscope for photographing or producing a representation of a spectrum.

STAGGARD, n. a four-year-old male red deer.

STANHOPE, n. a light, open, one-seated, horse-drawn carriage with two or four wheels.

STATUTORY, adj. of, pertaining to, or of the nature of a statute.

STENOTHERMAL, adj. *Ecol.* (of a plant or animal) able to withstand only slight variations in temperature.

STENOTHERMOPHILE, n. a stenothermophilic basterium.

STENOTOPIC, adj. *Ecol.* (of a plant or animal) able to tolerate only limited variations in conditions of the environment, as in temperature, humidity, etc.

STEREOGRAM, n. a diagram or picture representing objects in a way to give the impression of solidity.

STERNUTATION, n. act of sneezing.

STIGMATYPY, n. *Print.* the art or technique of making a design or portrait by combining small dots of various sizes.

STINK HORN, n. any of various rank-smelling, basidiomycetous fungi of the genus *Phallus*, esp. *P. impudicus*.

STONE CHAT, n. any of several small Old World thrushes, as *S. Torquata*.

SUBGUM, adj. *Chinese or Chinese-American Cookery.* prepared with mixed vegetables, as with water chestnuts, mushrooms, and bean sprouts.

SUCTORIAN, n. a protozoan of the class or order *Suctoria*.

SYLLABUB, n. a drink or dish made of milk or cream mixed with wine, cider or the like, often sweetened and flavored.

SYMPATHIN, n. *Biochem.* a hormone-like substance, secreted by sympathetic nerve endings, that serves to increase the heart rate, constrict the arterioles of the skin and mucous membranes, and dilate the arterioles of the skeletal and cardiac muscles.

T

TABLATURE, n. a tabular space, surface or structure.

TANGENT, adj. in immediate physical contact; touching.

TANGERINE, n. a small, loose-skinned variety of mandarin orange.

TARPAN, n. a wild horse, *Equus przewalskii*, of central Asia.

TECTRIX, n. *Ornith.* covert.

TELEPORT, v.t. to transport (a body) by telekinesis.

TEMPLET, n. a pattern, mold, or the like, usually consisting of a thin plate of wood or metal, serving as a gauge or guide in mechanical work.

TENTORIUM, n. (of an insect) the endoskeleton of the head.

THESAURUS, n. a reference book of synonyms and antonyms.

THYMINE, n. *Biochem.* a white, crystalline, water-insoluble pyrimidine, derived from thymus DNA, used chiefly in medical and biochemical research.

TITIVATE, v.t. titillate.

TITUBATION, n. *Pathol.* a disturbance of a body equilibrium in standing or walking, resulting in an uncertain gait and trembling, esp. resulting from diseases of the cerebellum.

TOURMALINE, n. a mineral, essentially a complex silicate containing boron, aluminum, etc., usually black but having various colored, transparent varieties used as gems.

TRIODE, n. *Electronics.* a vacuum tube containing three elements, usually plate, grid and cathode.

TRIPPANT, adj. *Heraldry.* (of a deer or the like) represented in the act of walking.

U

UMBRETTE, n. hammerhead.

UNMORTISE, v.t. to unfasten or separate (something mortised).

UNTOWARD, adj. unfavorable or unfortunate.

V

VARIOCOUPLER, n. *Elect.* a transformer having coils with a self-impedence that is essentially constant but a mutual impedence that can be varied by moving one coil with respect to the other.

VASTITY, n. *Archaic.* immensity; vastness.

VOTARY, n. a person who is bound by solemn religious vows, as a monk or nun.

W

WARSTLE, n. *Chiefly Scottish.* wrestle.

WHEELABRATE, v.t. to harden the surface of (steel) by bombarding it with a Wheelabrator.

WINDAGE, n. the influence of the wind in deflecting a missile.

WIND SUCKER, n. *Vet. Med.* a horse afflicted with cribbing.

WITHERITE, n. a white to grayish mineral, barium carbonate, occurring in crystals and masses: a minor ore of barium.

WONDERBERRY, n. the black, edible fruit of an improved garden variety of the black nightshade.

Y

YAMPEE, n. a herbaceous vine, *Dioscorea trifida,* of South America, having edible tubers.

YOKEFELLOW, n. an intimate associate; a partner.

Z

ZED-BAR, n. *Brit.* a metal bar with a Z-shaped section.